If I Only Had 25 Hours in a Day...

If I Only Had 25 Hours in a Day...

Melinda Turner

ACKNOWLEDGEMENTS

First, I want to thank God for all He has done in my life. I am so humbled and grateful to Him for His grace and mercy. All the glory and honor goes to Him.

Thanks to all the family and friends who helped make this book become real.

A special thank you to all who shared their amazing and anointed testimonies. God bless.

Thanks also to Alfreada Brown-Kelly, author of *Decrees and Declarations of Authenticity, Why Women Weep, The Skin I am In* and *Transformation of The Mind, Body & Soul.* I am so grateful for all your wise counsel in helping me bring these pages together to form *If I Only Had 25 Hours in a Day....*

TABLE OF CONTENTS

DEDICATION

This book is dedicated to my husband and son.

Love you guys so much.

INTRODUCTION

Life Waits for No One

"Why, you do not even know what will happen tomorrow. What is your life? You are a mist that appears for a little while and then vanishes."
James 4:14

" We need to get ready for the train, but I don't see it. Oh, wait a minute, there it is." Everybody is making their way toward the train. No one seems to be running, or rushing, just walking at a normal pace. I can see them as they start to board the train . I start to move toward the train and I say, " Wait a minute, there is something I

must do". I look around again, and the train is

pulling away. The train is leaving without me. I

am frozen in my thoughts. I am waiting,

waiting, waiting. Surely , someone on that train

will tell the conductor to stop. I know the train

will not leave without me. The train disappears.

There I stand, by myself, waiting, waiting,

waiting.

As I reflected back on this dream, I asked

myself, "What does this mean? God, what are

you trying to tell me? Is the train a symbol for

life? Am I missing life because I am too busy

doing something else? Focusing on the things in

this world, instead of life itself? Am I

depending on others to stop the train, to stop

life as it continues to move forward? Depending on others to make life wait for me? Maybe, it means it just wasn't my time to catch the train. Was it that plain and simple? NO, I don't think so. Somehow, I believe it was more than that."

We need to see life as that moving train. It appears as scheduled, but we only have so much time, making frequent stops on this journey called life and then it is gone before we know it. Somehow we expect life to wait on us until we are ready to catch that train. Do we just sit around and wait for the next train to maybe come, or receive the gift of life that is here and now? What if there was not another train, what if we missed the only train that would take us where we needed to go?

I believe we all have a purpose in life that God has designed for us, and He provides the what, the how, the where, and the when. Don't let life leave you behind because you may be missing out on what God has planned for you.

Along with my story, I hope you will also be inspired by others who have shared their amazing testimonies.

 **Chapter 1**

Are you Living or Existing?

There you go again... looking at your watch.

Looking at the clock. Not looking at the clock.

So much to do, with so little time. You know the

saying...places to go, people to see and things to

do.

No, I may not know who you are, but I know me.

And that was me a "minute" ago. No pun

intended. Not 60 seconds ago, as we know it to

be, but a time period in my life when I felt hard-

pressed on every side and under pressure to

stay in control of my life when, slowly, I saw it slipping away.

I thank you and appreciate the fact that you have taken a minute to pick up this book. Already you have taken the first step in your change process. Time is so precious in our busy lives that we do not have that extra one minute to spare. We take for granted that there will always be a tomorrow or the next day. I know, because so many, many, of us including myself have felt that same way.

Remember the time when you walked in the living room and forgot the reason you went there? Or the time when you were driving to the grocery store, and passed your destination?

What about the times you wake up in the mornings, and want to return back to bed because you already know how hectic the day will be? How about waking up not knowing whether it is Tuesday or Wednesday because the days are passing by so fast? Been there, done that, got the T-shirt. No, I was not having memory issues, I was having *more-than- I could-handle* issues. Too many things to do, not enough time. We are in constant motion, but amazingly enough, somehow we are not getting anywhere.

How many times have we said this to ourselves, "*If only I had that extra hour*?" What would I do with that extra 60 minutes a day?

We convince ourselves on a daily basis that the reason we cannot finish what we start is because of not enough time in a day. Here is some food for thought... what if time or lack of it is not the answer to our problem, but changing the problem itself is the answer.

I took that question to a few of my friends and as you will see, there were various sorts of replies. They were people of different occupations, different ages, different lifestyles, who could relate to the problem.

Gloria said, "More time to relax or get in more exercise, or just be still and pray."

Sharon gave this reply, "To truly find and cultivate my passion... to truly enjoy life."

Monique stated, "Read, write, and create".

Rhonda had this to say, "Pray, and spend more time in the flower bed."

Rae simply stated, "Just need more 'me' time and exercise."

Christine answered the question with one word, "Sleep."

Spenser gave it some thought and replied, "Spend time with family and my pup!"

One participant could not give me an answer, because she stated one hour was not enough. I know the list could go on and on.

Take a minute to answer the question for

yourself. What would you do with that extra

hour in a day?

* * *

If we look at the answers from this small group

sample, can we conclude that that one extra

hour would be spent on providing us with more

time to focus on ourselves, from praying more to just sleeping more. Amazingly enough, how easy it is to place our needs behind everything and everyone else. This leads me to another question. Are we living or existing? What is the difference? Are they not the same? Yes, I believe there is a difference. My thoughts are that when we are truly living, we enjoy our lives. We are grateful for all of God's blessings. No matter what the world tries to throw at us, we can at the end of the day still say I love my life and thank God for everything in it. Existing as defined the American Heritage Dictionary means "to live at a minimal level; subsist" and "to continue to be." Are we just doing only what we need to get by until the next day?

One quote from a famous philosopher and founder of the Colony of Pennsylvania , William Penn (1644-1718), "Time is what we want most, but what we use worst" makes a great point. Can we utilize our time in a more productive way? Can we do things we enjoy and still find the time to live a productive life?

We all know that time stops for no one. On the contrary, we practice the tradition of advancing our clocks one hour ahead during the summer for Daylight Saving's Time. We experience longer days and shorter nights. Unfortunately, the opposite occurs in the winter months, when we shift our clocks back one hour. Without getting into a discussion of the how and why it happens, relating to the earth and sun, my point is the one hour we think we have gained we eventually lose. I, personally, sleep through it. Now we are back to where we started: those continued cycles of years, days, hours, minutes, seconds.

Now can *I* give you that extra hour? Can *I* tell you how to find that extra hour?

No, I cannot. But what I can do is share my story of how I learned to live a life where I understood how to enjoy and love the time God blessed me with and not just existed. Trying to place 25 hours in a 24-hour day was trying to do the impossible, so I had to make a change.

As you read other testimonies throughout this

book, they also faced challenges, trials and

tribulations in their journey called life, but came

out the victor.

 **Chapter 2**

He Speaks to Me

The idea for this book took shape about a year ago. I was encouraged seeing how my life had changed from days filled with stress and the battle within to make a change. For too long, I tried to fight an enemy all by myself. My worldly thinking lead me to believe I had it all under control. It was not until I realized the only One who had control was God. I needed and wanted to live a life with purpose and peace. My life is not perfect by any means, but it is such a blessing to say I am not who and

where I used to be. I wanted to be able to
share with others who had to cope with some
of the same challenges I faced and how I
conquered those mountains.

When I look back over my life, I remember as a
young child growing up in a large family, I was
taught to be strong, independent, nurturing, and
giving of myself. Determined from an early age
in life, I was going to be self-sufficient, self-
reliant, and self-sustaining. I graduated from
high school and progressed with my nursing
degree in hand and I set out on my journey to
save the world. That's who I was, someone who
cared for people, looked after, ministered to
their needs at no matter the cost. I took on

more than I could handle, but now I realize that my job was not to save, help, and rescue everyone and everything. I thought my life was fulfilled with my professional career and some added activities that I squeezed in. I also enjoyed baking, which eventually became another full- time occupation. I had no idea that the day would come when I had to make a change. After 15 years of waking up every morning starting a new day and maintaining the same ritual, I slowly added more and more things to my daily routine. In retrospect, I know now what the cost was...me.

My sanity, my family, my peace and my closeness with God was the cost. I was trying to exist in a way that would eventually bring about depression, guilt, anger, and regret.

It's been two years since I decided to make the changes I needed in my life to start living again. I'm still going through trials, but I'm coming out even stronger from the lessons I learned. Thank God for my testimony, because it brought me closer to Him.

2 Timothy 3:16-17 *All Scripture is God-breathed and is useful for teaching, rebuking, correcting and training in righteousness. so that the man of God may be thoroughly equipped for every good work.*

Not knowing how to get started placing my thoughts to paper, I prayed to God for guidance and direction. He gave me a spirit of discernment. He spoke an idea that would soon take shape. I realize through our circumstances we learn life lessons. It is when we share our testimonies with others that we find growth and understanding and healing; these benefits are not only for ourselves, but for others.

I replied to God, "When will I find the time to write this book?" The answer for me was...

Ecclesiastes 3-22 *Wherefore I perceive that there is nothing better, than that a man should rejoice in his own works: for that is his portion:*

for who shall bring him to see what shall be after him.

As I began to write, I knew my intent for this book was to help someone make a change in their life for the good. As with everything in life, expectations bring disappointments. We assume things should happen in a certain way because we see it that way . Do not let one or two setbacks deter you from your victory. Many lessons are learned through our own designs and misdesigns. Again, we need to realize we are not in control.

Isaiah 55:8 *"For my thoughts are not your thoughts, neither are your ways my ways,"* *declared the Lord.*

Expecting to write this book, I thought it would be easy. This was a very humbling experience. There were many days and nights not knowing what to say or how to say it. I would allow feelings of uncertainty and apprehension to fill my thoughts. But if you put your trust in the Lord, as I did, you can overcome that negative thinking. I kept pressing on, and the words would soon come together.

Proverbs 16:3 *Commit your work to the Lord, and your plans will be established.*

Walk with me through my journey of change. My steps may not be your steps. Every chapter may not be your chapter. But, I believe that there is something for you in this book that will help you to decide to make the changes that are required for you to live your best life. It was and still is a perpetual process, never-ending. A set of steps we all need to go through, but with prayer and wise counsel I have found positive and meaningful direction in my life.

Ecclesiastes 2:24 *A person can do nothing better than to eat and drink and find satisfaction in their own toil. This too, I see, is from the hand of God.*

God wants us to have a life where we rejoice in our work, understanding that this is a gift from God. He wants us to lead a prosperous and productive life.

I encourage you to take *time* out your busy day as you read this book to look at your life and your gifts. I challenge you to remove all doubts and fears that you may have about change, because where there is change, there is growth and learning. You must have faith to start the journey of *really* living.

Testimony of Faith

The Conversion Experience

In September of 2008 at 35 years of age, I was deployed to Kirkuk, Iraq with my Air Force unit. My wife was six months pregnant at the time, and I departed home the day Hurricane Gustav came ashore. The storm eventually caused damage in our county and to our home. Leaving my family was a mental challenge in itself but the added actions of Mother Nature made this deployment one of epic proportions. But it was at that time in my life where I experienced a very special period in my life. I developed closeness with God like never before.

During the deployment, I decided to fully trust God more than others, including myself. I experienced God's presence in a very mighty way and was left in awe of God's love and goodness. I prayed more than ever during the 110 days I was deployed. There was no guarantee that I would make it home safe and sound or in time for the birth of my child but I kept praying. God made a way for me to return home in time for the delivery and I will be forever grateful to Him for His kindness in that regard. Ever since that time in my life, I have become a true believer that He can make the impossible possible and the unbeliever a believer. Amen.

Minister Charles E. Harkless, Jr.
Retired United States Air Force (2012)

 **Chapter 3**

Making the Change

Philippians 4:6-7 *Do not be anxious about anything, but in everything, by prayer and petition, with thanksgiving, present your request to God. And the peace of God, which transcends all understanding, will guard your hearts and your minds in Christ Jesus.*

Everybody's red flag is different. Everybody's low point in life is different. Everybody will experience their own trials and tribulations. What is for me is for me and what is for you is for you. We are faced with a lot of obstacles that prevent us from finding that inner peace in our life. So many worldly stressors and stresses can take hold of our thoughts. But, we must be mindful of why we do certain things. Is it really for the good of others or is it for our own self-gratification? Are we secretly enjoying the attention that we receive from the world? Do we believe that the best rewards are those that are external and not internal?

In James 1:14, the word reads *But each person is tempted when he is lured and enticed by his own desire.*

We are reminded of the story of the sisters Martha and Mary from Scripture (Luke 10:38-42). Many can relate to Martha, who is known for being a hard worker, giving of herself. She is always trying to get things done, making sure everything is perfect and in order. I definitely could see myself in that way. I made sure if the work didn't get done by someone else, I did it myself. Delegating was never one of my strengths. Why ask or tell someone else to do something, when in the end it may not get done, or it may not be done in your time? What if it is not done the way you want it done? Why waste time thinking about all the "ifs" when you could just do it yourself?

When I would invite guests over, my whole focus was making sure I had the right food, the right conversation, the right decorations, the right everything. That became a hallmark of mine by many; expecting the familiarity of my hospitality. I found myself always in the kitchen, never really enjoying the pleasant company of others.

Now, as we recall the story, Jesus was to visit Bethany and visited Martha and Mary's home. They were true followers of the Son of God and His ministry. As we fast forward, we see Martha busily preparing for her guest and making sure everything was in order. Was table set, the food just right? Was the family ready? When Jesus arrived, He was truly greeted with warmth and love by all. Martha continued to be busy at her duties that she believed were most important.

While looking upon her guests, Martha saw her sister Mary sitting at Jesus' feet listening attentively to His every word. Mary was receiving all the wisdom and knowledge that Jesus shared with all His disciples.

Now Martha became upset with Mary and her attention was no longer on serving others and Jesus, but on herself. She was feeling that Mary should be helping her, instead of doing "nothing". But as we come to realize, Mary knew the true importance of Jesus' visit and Martha lost sight of that. Soon pride reared its ugly head when Martha should have humbled herself. As Martha shared her grievance with

Jesus of her thoughts about Mary, Martha was surprised at His answer.

Luke 10:38-42 *(KJV) Now it came to pass, as they went, that he entered into a certain village: and a certain woman named Martha received him into her house.*

And she had a sister called Mary, which also sat at Jesus' feet, and heard his word.

But Martha was cumbered about much serving, and came to him, and said, Lord, dost thou not care that my sister hath left me to serve alone? bid her therefore that she help me.

And Jesus answered and said unto her, Martha, Martha, thou art careful and troubled about many things:

But one thing is needful: and Mary hath chosen

that good part, which shall not be taken away

from her.

How can you relate this story to your everyday life? To your job, your home life, your school life? Are we more like Martha or Mary? Are we self-serving or people-serving? Are these things that upset you more important than the "good part" of life? Do you spend more time doing the preparation and the work than enjoying your company?

I can relate. Too many times, I focused on the external (the world) things. I was making sure my house was in order, making sure the chores were done and making sure the family was ready. Too often I was thinking all these things were the most important when I should have focused on the internal (the heart and the spirit). *The Lord does not look at the things people look at. People look at the outward appearance, but the Lord looks at the heart.* 1 Samuel 16:7

Changes take many forms.

Testimony of Change

The Serenity Prayer made famous by the late Reinhold

Niebuhr (1892-1971) says, "God grant me the serenity

to accept the things I cannot change, courage to change

the things I can, and the wisdom to know the

difference." Change is a very integral part of our daily

walk with God. Each day gives birth to its own set of

challenges, trials and tribulations; you have to be

'prayed up' to be flexible enough to change and cope

with what life has in store for us daily.

When I think of change, I am reminded of the Biblical

story of Lazarus in John Chapter 11. Many Bible readers

and churchgoers are very familiar with that particular

story. The synopsis is that Lazarus was sick, then he

died, then Jesus raised him from the dead. While doing

some exegetical study on the story, I picked up on

something. When Lazarus died, his sisters Mary and

Martha immediately looked at the situation closely. They became very emotional because Jesus had taken His time getting there. They were like "Lord, if You would have just stepped in at the right time, this change for the worse wouldn't have happened". We at times may ask ourselves that same question, " Lord if only...?" We may have the same reaction. But the Lord sometimes will allow change and the negative situation to materialize and there is a good reason why. When the situation was fixed it was obvious that nobody else but the Lord could have fixed this. It certainly did not fix itself. God receives all the glory.

On another aspect of change, I enrolled in Seminary bible college after retiring from the Air Force. Years ago, my pastor who is my father told me to be on guard for a change. I knew exactly what he meant by that now. Believe it or not, Satan will do what he can to try to change the direction of a child of God. Some of the strangest things happened in my life immediately after I had enrolled in school. Controversial and trivial things that had never happened before in my life surfaced. Satan knows what is dear to our hearts and what we love, and he will often try to use that against us in order to create division and a spirit of discouragement in our lives. It could be your children, parents or it may even be your brother or your sister.

I remember my grandmother saying to someone many years ago, "God allows things to happen sometimes so that we can get a testimony out of it so that Jesus can fix it for you". I am thankful that we have a loving and merciful God in our life. Sometimes we may get emotional like Mary and Martha because of our care and concern for our family, and for a split second we can take our eyes off Jesus, make a mistake and lose our faith. But as the story of Lazarus ends, God will always show up and show how He makes it right.

Reinhold Niebuhr said it best when he also stated,

"Living one day at a time;

enjoying one moment at a time;

accepting hardships as the pathway to peace;

taking, as He did, this sinful world

as it is, not as I would have it;

trusting that He will make all things right

if I surrender to His Will;

that I may be reasonably happy in this life

and supremely happy with Him

forever in the next."

Amen.

Minister Charles E. Harkless, Jr.
Retired United States Air Force (2012)

 **Chapter 4**

No Time to Cry

I reflected back on those days when the stressors of mine were getting me down. I tried too often to "Be all, do all and complete all". My days were chaotic with too many things going on at one time. Feelings of disappointments, fear, sadness, depression and not enough of joy filled my life. I felt my *bad* days did outweigh my *good* days!

It is almost impossible to give the best of yourself when you have lost yourself in the midst of all you do. Trying to divide your time and energy into many undertakings meant you were not giving the whole you to any of them. This superwoman attitude did not take place over night. It was an ongoing process. I can recall one of my sisters saying that I was the go-to person if you needed help or guidance because I had a maturity that made you think I was the oldest and not the youngest of seven children in the family. I found myself never knowing how to say "No, I cannot, I do not know", because I always tried to find an answer.

I remember the time when my mom was very ill and doctors' appointments became frequent. I chose to drive her to her appointments knowing there would be consequences on my job.

Instead of looking for options, I made it my responsibility to get her there. Again, that giving of oneself and that nursing instinct was what made me continue to do what I do. But, in the end I can remember her words, thanking me for all I had done and letting me know I had done enough. I think she was trying to tell me that I cannot do it all.

When I posed the question to myself, *What would I do with an extra hour a day?* it was not easy to be honest with myself. That meant I had to take off the armor, and let down my guard. I knew the answer to that question would be something that many could not understand...

I replied, "I would cry". I did not give myself time to cry. No time to clear my eyes of all the "junk" I carried. It was a luxury I could not afford. How could I not have time to cry? Most people associate crying with an involuntary process, something you do and not have to think about. I was so much wanting to keep "it" (meaning my life) all together that crying was not part of the process. I kept it all inside. Realizing that was my choice, I had to own up to it. I believe myself to be a strong person able to take on any challenge that comes my way. The problem with that is when everyone else sees you as being strong, no one asks if *you* are ok? We all need to cry sometimes because it is a natural process and a way to release our

sadness or our joy.

Psalm 126:5 *Those who sow in tears shall reap*

with shouts of joy!

I wanted my joy back! I wanted my peace back!

I wanted my sanity back! I wanted and needed

to recover them all!

In the medical field, there is another kind of

recovery. Going through a procedure, a patient

may be placed under some type of anesthesia.

The purpose of the anesthesia is to numb the

senses so he or she will not feel anything. Once

the anesthesia starts to wear off, it was my job

to make sure that my patient was stable.

I needed to make sure his breathing was not labored, his blood pressure not too high, nor not too low, his pulse at a normal rate, and his pain was manageable. When I looked back at my life, my stress became my anesthesia. I did not feel all the pressure I was putting on myself while allowing all the negativity of the world and pain to weigh me down.

It numbed me so I could not feel all the good things that God had planned for me. Now, when you get to that point in your life, it is definitely time to make a *change.* That was my wakeup call! I had to break the chain that held me tied.

For many, change does not take place overnight. It is a growth experience.

Testimony of Growth

My name is Ashley, I'm 29 years old as of now. This has surely been a long road... finding myself and loving every little bit God has made of me as He continues to fill me!

I started out a great kid, one that loved everyone and everything in life! Appreciating life for what it's worth I had a family life that was full of complete blessings.. full of fun & love & laughter!! Lots of special moments were included over the years... with ALL sides of the family! Nothing has thankfully ever changed..

Through my school years, I was a rather attentive child, ready to learn, and getting decent grades . I loved everyone and of course was friends with everyone! When I graduated to junior high, I met all different sorts of people. I was slightly a little bit shyer. By the time I hit ninth grade I wanted the guys to like me; I wanted to be cool! I was kind of a chubby little girl, but big into playing sports. Very active in my neighborhood riding bikes & walking with friends playing some type of ball. The good and simple life looking back, all used to develop me into who I am today. Gradually, as I got to a few school dances, I found myself going on my own, no date. At first it was ok, danced with a friend or two. Slow dancing with my girl friends a lot too, but as years progressed, it would not be enough! I still held my head proud though. I was a strong woman, I had my guy friends, my "padnas!" With close friends comes maturity!

Well eventually times got different and the cool thing to do was being bad... sneaking out of the house, stealing cigarettes and beers occasionally while walking the neighborhood! It was silly. That went on for a few years... and then drugs came into play. As a teenager, I experimented with weed. Of course we loved it... it was so cool!..so we thought.

That has been my major weakness through the years... trying to be cool, trying to fit in places the God in me had no place being. I started with the drinking and drugs getting a little closer to guys... I always kind of wanted that! I was friends with everyone but wanted more. Even though I made the grades, I ended up getting expelled! I had been hanging out with the wrong crowd. I was in ninth grade; I should have been setting an example for the kids in seventh and eighth grades. But I didn't, I just went along with the crowd. So many are caught up and sucked into that trap today the devil puts out! It's a crying shame to see so many others flushing their lives down the drain, wasting so many years of their lives that could have molded them into a more well-rounded follower! But at the same time, looking back this was exactly the plan God has molded since I took that wrong turn in life! I feel God was telling

me, "I have constructed a plan for you"...to be continued.

Ashley

 **Chapter 5**

The Faces of Depression

Yes, I tried to accomplish the impossible. Yes, I tried to fit 25 hours of work in a 24-hour period. Tired, exhausted, and broken is when the enemy saw the perfect time to enter into my life. As I look back over my life, God had given me all the warning signs. I wasn't listening to His voice and I wasn't seeing the warning signs. The stumbling blocks were there to slow me down. My husband would tell me "You cannot continue to work on 3 hours of sleep a night". I was trying to work two jobs along with

everything else that goes into being a wife and
mother. As long as I was functioning, getting
the work done, I found a way around all the ups
and downs and continued on that unsafe path.
It did not happen overnight, I struggled to live
this impossible schedule I created for years,
because when I made a commitment, I followed
through. I would wake-up mornings not
thinking but just doing. I would not stop until I
went to bed that night or morning, whatever
the case. Then one day, I ran straight into that
wall that I call depression.   Like a ton of bricks
it came tumbling down on me. I could not go left
or right. I could not go over it or under it. I had
to go through it. I looked at my life and saw

sadness. I saw my son growing up before my eyes. I felt regret for not seeing what my husband had warned me about. I lost focus on what was important; God and family.

Who do you see? You see what I allow you to see. Man sees the external and not the internal, the heart. Most of us do not wear the letter 'D' for depression to acknowledge to everyone what we are going through, because it has the stigma of weakness. Like a robot, we just do what we do, and move on. There are many faces of depression. It is not always sadness. For some people depression is hidden behind the laughter. We try to joke ourselves out of the real issues that we cannot cope with.

Depression can be revealed in your attitude. You are always finding the negative in life, when the positive is staring you right in the face. You are always looking at the glass half-empty, instead of half-full. You are always asking, "Why me, Lord?" instead of asking "What is this lesson I need to learn?" There is a spiritual depression. You are conflicted over your faith. You feel hopeless because you have forgotten all the goodness that Lord has done for you. I know that my faith in man was wrongly placed. More often than not, disappointments follow every expectation. There are times you feel lonely when you are in crowded room, trying to make everyone happy which we know to be impossible. We cannot please everyone... only ourselves. Another face of depression is waking up just to exist and having no sense of direction in your life. You cannot find any reason to keep moving from day to day. In other words, you have no purpose in life. Depression comes also in the face of anger. You are looking for answers from the world, and the world is turning its back on you. You just cannot find understanding on how to live a life of peace.

At first, I didn't have time to cry, but now I am crying all the time; not from gladness, but because I am sad. I feel such an emptiness, regret, shame and guilt over how many years I wasted not seeing my blessings. I was not being grateful for my many gifts the Lord has allowed me to have, asking too many times "Why, Lord?" I knew the only way out of this downward spiral was to look up. I knew a change had to come. I knew my faith had to be *renewed* and *redirected.*

"For I know the plans I have for you", declares the Lord, "plans to prosper you and not to harm you, plans to give you hope and a future. Then you will call upon Me and come and pray to Me, and I will listen to you. You will seek Me and find Me when you seek Me with all your heart."
Jeremiah 29:11-13

When I made that commitment to serve God and look to Him from where comes my help, I knew I could get through that wall that the enemy had placed in front of me and come out stronger. *Yet I am always with you; you hold me by my right hand.* Psalm 73:23

My eyes were opened to all the things I could not see. Purpose and the meaning of purpose was placed in my life. I took back my family, my peace, and my choice because the world didn't give it to me. When we submit to God, we find a change within. We find a spiritual strength that can fight any battle and know the victory is ours.

Testimony of Submission

Submit to God and be at peace with him; in this way prosperity will come to you. Accept instruction from his mouth and lay up his words in your heart. If you return to the Almighty, you will be restored: if you remove wickedness far from your tent and assign your nuggets to the dust, your gold of Ophir to the rocks in the ravines, then the Almighty will be your gold, the choicest silver for you. Surely then you will find delight in the Almighty and will lift up your face to God. Job 22:21-26

I was depressed, stressed, and hard pressed on every side and I needed some type of order in my life. Too busy for God, my family, for me. I had too much pride to ask for help, believing the things of the world could bring me joy and happiness. I was looking in all the wrong directions for my peace of mind. My plans were not His plans and my will, not His will. I did not know what to do anymore. I couldn't eat because my appetite was gone. I had many sleepless nights where I just waited for the hours to pass. My family was slipping away. I saw myself changing not only on the outside, but on the inside. Suddenly one Saturday morning, I surrendered all. I made that change. "Lord, I submit to You." No longer do I ask "Why me Lord?" I say, "Why not me, Lord, let Your will be done. For You know what is best for me. Use me Lord as Thy humbled servant." God, family, and all else will follow. My blessings come from the Word, and there is power in Thy Word.

Hebrews 4:12-13 *For the word of God is quick, and powerful, and sharper than any two-edged sword, piercing even to the dividing asunder of soul and spirit, and of the joints and marrow, and is a discerner of the thoughts and intents of the heart. Neither is there any creature that is not manifest in his sight: but all things are naked and opened unto the eyes of him with whom we have to do.*

Now, my *good* days outweigh my *bad* days, and I won't complain. I have purpose, and joy in my heart. Praises go up for blessings to come down. Now I can profess that all that I have is a gift from God. And I am so thankful for His grace and mercy. Many times when I wanted to say no and give up, God said yes.

Proverbs 3:5-6 *Trust in the Lord with all your heart and lean not on your own understanding. In all your ways submit to Him, and He will make your paths straight.*

The plans He has for me I receive and believe!

Melinda

 **Chapter 6**

Slow Down or Life Will Pass You By

When I submitted and gave my worry to God, that did not mean all my work was done. It was only the beginning of a whole new journey. I continued to work through my trial and come out stronger and wiser. I had to listen and pay closer attention to what God all the while was trying to show me. As I made the changes in my life, I now know I needed to be patient and trust Him.

Mark 6:31 *Then, because so many people were coming and going that they did not even have a chance to eat, he said to them, "Come with me by*

yourselves to a quiet place and get some rest."

We never know how, when and where wise

counsel will be entrusted in our lives. We must

be ready at any given moment to receive it. We

wait for God's message to come to us like a

roaring lion, or written across the sky. But God

speaks to us quietly and often through others. I

previously shared that my husband encouraged

me to slow down, and my mother stated I had

done enough. There were probably many

others that I just did not hear because I just did

not take the time to listen.

 I had never met this person before, nor did I

know her name. But, as I know now, there is no

such thing as coincidence. I believe we are destined to be in the right place, at the right time; people are brought in our lives for a reason as you will later read on my travels to Tennessee.

Proverbs 12:15 *The way of fools seems right to them, but the wise listens to advice.*

I was at the register one Saturday afternoon, checking out at my second favorite place (first being attending church), a well-known shopping center. I could hear the cashier telling me my total. Apparently, it was not her first time saying the amount, because I was so engrossed in thinking about what I had to do next, I did not hear her speaking to me.

I told her, "I'm sorry, I was so busy in my mind, I was not paying attention." I shared with her that I must have been thinking about what I needed to do next. She looked at me and responded, "You need to slow down or life will pass you by."

Not really knowing what that meant, I smiled, agreed, and answered, Yes, I know." I received her wisdom and paid my bill and continued on my journey. As I was driving home, I started thinking about what the friendly cashier had told me, "Slow down or life will pass you by." What did that mean?

"Don't have time for that", came to mind. So I dismissed what she said.

Days passed, maybe even weeks. But, when I was back in that store again, my thoughts came back to that time at the register and what the friendly cashier had advised. I don't know when it happened, but I figured it out!

I was not living in the present time, but living in the future. I was not seeing what was right in front of me, but looking always ahead. I was not living for today, but only existing to move to the next task.

She was right. As society engages us to keep moving forward, we have programmed ourselves to keep thinking ahead so as not to be "left behind".

Hello!

It's a start, y'all. I'll try to slow down my mind. I'll take some deep breaths. I will make the effort to take in my surroundings. I will take a minute to look at what is right in front of me. I will 'own' my here and now. I will take control and claim it. What does all that mean? It means I will live one minute at a time, one hour at a time, one day at a time. Do not take for granted when your life starts to turn around that you can go back to your old ways. Acknowledge what God had done for you, and be thankful.

Testimony of Gratitude

At the age of 24, I began drinking beer. I was functioning well at work and maintaining a job and apartment. Later my drinking became a habit and got worse. I would work and could not wait to get off to get a beer. This went on for years. I was to the point that I was missing work for weeks at a time. It got so bad that I lost my apartment, but God was merciful and supplied me with another job and a place to live. I got comfortable with what I had, so instead of being grateful I continued in my sin (drinking). I drank until one day I was stricken with a grand mal seizure. This is where you lose consciousness and have violent muscle contractures. God rescued me and I have been grateful ever since. I got saved in August 2003 and have been free from alcohol ever since that day. I thank God for having mercy on me and delivering me from alcohol. Now I can get up every morning praising God for allowing me to feel good in my body and in my right

mind. I owe all this to the glory of God.

G. B.

 **Chapter 7**

I Feel Like I Can Never Catch Up (or Get Ahead)

Ever had that feeling when you think you are the only one who sees certain things? Let me explain.

When you walk in the house after a long day of 'busyness', why is it only you who see those dishes in the sink? Is it only you who sees that unmade bed? Who is going to help the kids with the homework? I think I need to go grocery shopping.

I remember a time when I thought I was "caught up". I had the chores done, the shopping completed and whatever else I had planned for that day. Finding a moment in time to talk to my friend, I made a phone call. We started talking about various topics, and I commented that I accomplished a lot today. And her reply was, "*And now you are looking for something to dust*". Oh my, she knew me too well.

I would come home from a long day of working and would find myself getting angry, first at myself, then at my family. Of course, I never intended to throw blame or ill feelings toward them. The enemy was opening that door, and I stepped right through it.

In John 10:10 *The thief comes only to steal and kill and destroy; I have come that they may have life, and it to the full.*

Frustrated with myself, I projected my anger and guilt on to the people who were the closest to me. Like *a thief, I almost destroyed* the love of my family. When I could not complete everything I had assigned myself, it meant failure. Let me repeat that I had *assigned* myself. Another *change* had to come.

I believe we tend to place ourselves in situations where we cannot win the battle because we continue to fight with the wrong weapons.

2 Corinthians 10:4 *The weapons we fight with are not the weapons of the world. On the contrary, they have divine power to demolish strongholds.*

When we try to take on the world by ourselves using our emotions, we feel obligated to do everything we need to do to get the job done, whether it is a "specific duty, role, or function." We are mother, father, friend, co-worker, counselor, etc.

My word of the day: Epiphany...*a moment in which you suddenly see or understand something in a new or very clear way.*

Only I was responsible for the stress that I placed upon myself It's human nature that contributes to us feeling indispensable. We have that 'can do it all attitude' in our lives. The burden is too much. Our mind, body and spirit are not designed to carry such a heavy load.

Matthew 11:28 *" Come to Me, all you who are weary and burdened, and I will give you rest."*

As I came to realize Who really was in control, and that it was not me, I had to make some hard decisions. I had to decide what to do and what not to do. As we place importance on our life's duties, we must learn to prioritize.

Oh, this may sound so simple, or maybe not, but for me it was a struggle. I know I am not alone out there. I had to relinquish that control. We are always trying to get ahead, catch up, or finish something. Why? just so we can start something else we overbook ourselves to do. Just like a hotel, there are only so many rooms we can fill. Just like so many hours in a day, there are just only so many things we can do in those hours. We have only so much space in our brain, until we get overloaded. Then our decision- making is affected. We are easily distracted. We cannot focus on what we are doing. Ask yourself..What are we trying to get ahead of, or trying to catch up? Maybe, I just didn't dust enough, or cook enough, work

enough, or pray enough? How did I make that

change? I started small, one thing at a time.

 **Chapter 8**

Make a List, Then Remove Two Items.

James 4:6 *God opposes the proud but shows favor to the humble.*

As my day started, I tried to make a list of what my day would consist of. Well, in my head, my list of things I needed to do was attainable. I never really took a number count, and certainly never took into consideration the amount of time it would take for each task to be completed. I just committed myself to the job. I knew what I had to do and that I had to get it done. I can remember my husband would tell me always, "Melinda, you have no sense of time. You can't do all that." But I would ignore his wise counsel and say to myself," Yes I can." That was my pride speaking. I later learned pride only brings about destruction.

Proverbs 16:18 *Pride goes before destruction, a haughty spirit before a fall.* I was not taking into account that the time I used to complete all my tasks meant I had to take away my family time, sleep time, the quiet time, one-on-one I needed to spend with God. Maybe I could skip lunch, that could give me an extra hour. I'll stop exercising. I'll talk to my friends less. Does that sound familiar? Everybody's *things* are different, and everybody makes their own sacrifices. As I changed, my list making changed.

I actually had to write it down, pen to paper in hand, not just in my mind. I estimated the amount of time it took to do each assignment. Now, I was pretty sure I could do one , two, three, or even four things in a day. But could I do six or seven? No way. So when I made my list for the day, I first prioritized them by *real* importance. Then anything over four, I removed. It was not easy but at the end of the day, it was really rewarding. Many people may say, 'oh I can complete five or six' and I agree. Everybody's timing is different. But if it takes away my quiet time with God, my family time, and my me time, I remove something off the list. It is not worth the price and the stress and the loss of my peace of mind. Each day the numbers on your list may change, more or less. As of course as life happens, things may change depending on what you have planned for the day.

I had to learn to adjust my schedule for unforeseen circumstances. I had to be flexible. As Benjamin Franklin wrote in a 1789 letter "Our new Constitution is now established, and has an appearance that promises permanency; but in this world *nothing* can be certain, except *death* and *taxes*."

Another mountain I had to conquer was asking for help. No one can do it like me? Right? Again, I am in agreement. No one can do house chores like me. No one can do my job at work like me. I had to realize that no one does anything the same. But it does not make it wrong, just different. So I had to swallow that pride and ask for help and admit that I could not do it all. Now, I am accomplishing two things: first, I am decreasing the time to get these things done and second, I am increasing my time to do what is more important in my life.

Proverbs 11:2 *When pride comes, then comes disgrace, but with humility comes wisdom.*

The secret of my to-do list is to always place something that you enjoy on it. You will never feel a sense of fulfillment if *you* are not included in your happiness and sense of peace.

For me, my list always includes my quiet time with God. I realize my personal relationship with Him is above all else. I know He is the source to get through today, and the next day. There is nothing like family. Blood relatives may define as family, but the people I choose to be part of my life are also my family. Always have positive people in your life to share in your joy, and give you words of encouragement. Life is too short and precious to surround yourself with all the negativity of the world. It wears and tears you down. I will always find time for the people who I love and love me. Whatever can bring you to that place of contentment, include it on your list. Remember back when you answered the question..." What to do with that extra hour?" Include that answer on your list.

Watching your favorite television show may be on your list. I will share with you mine is Perry Mason. The best criminal attorney television has to offer, in my opinion. No insanity, just thought provoking entertainment. The irony of this is that I usually fall asleep before the courtroom scene is over. But, nevertheless, at the end of the day, it is one of my ways to wind down. Exercise will also be on my to-do list. As you may already know, exercise is not only a positive direction for a healthy lifestyle, it is also a way to reduce stress. Research has shown regular exercise can lead to preventing anxiety and feelings of depression. It can also increase self-esteem. Being of service to the community may be on that to-do list. There is nothing like that feeling of good works.

1 Peter 4:10 *Each of you should use whatever gift you have received to serve others, as faithful stewards of God's grace in its various forms.*

Journaling can be a wonderful way to reflect and examine your daily thoughts. Writing about the ins and outs of your day can bring about some insight to your life. How did I spend my day? Did I use my time wisely; what could have I done differently? Did I focus on the good, and not the bad? Did I live positively and not negatively? I place a book next to my bed at night and journal my many blessings and personal testimonies.

Psalm 51:10 *Create in me a clean heart, O God; and renew a right spirit within me.*

This is an ongoing process with a lot of trial and error. There is no right or wrong way, and it's OK. You really have to give yourself permission to stumble sometimes. Most importantly, remember that tomorrow is a new day. Do not give up. Try adding listening to music and meditating to your list. They are great ways to release stress and tension. Music has been known to be soothing for the soul and meditation is a process where we learn to exercise our mind. William Congreve (1670-1729) an English playwright and poet is famous for his quote "Music has charms to soothe the savage breast, to soften rocks or bend a knotted oak."

 **Chapter 9**

My Son Was One Year Old, Now He is a Teenager

Psalm 127:3 *Children are a heritage from the Lord, offspring a reward from him.*

One day, I was taller, gazing downward to see my son's face. Then, another day, my son and I were standing shoulder to shoulder, eye to eye. Now, he is 5-feet 8-inches, and I'm 5-feet 4-inches. Oh my, he is so tall. When did this happen?

It was 4:30am and some days 3:30am when the alarm clock went off. It was time to get up to go to work. Not being a morning person, I would struggle to get out of bed Getting ready, I would make it just in time to leave at the appropriate time so as not to be late for work. But, before I left, I would take that not so extra minute and quietly go to my son's room just to see his face before I left to start my day. While my son was still asleep, I was careful not to wake him. I just needed to check on him and make sure he was safe even though I knew his dad was only a few feet away. Sometimes, for some unknown reason he would open his eyes and see my face and return to sleep. I would ask him, at the end of the day, "Do you remember me going in your room?" Most of the time he said no. He would ask me, "Mom why do come in my room before you leave? "Because that's what I do," I would tell him, and smile.

Here are two stories I would love to share with you that I hope bring a smile to your face as they did to mine while I was writing them:

I was picking my son up from school one day. Like every day I asked, "How was your day?" as he looked at me with a look of dismay. He said, "Momma, I fell today." My eyes widened with a look of concern and I asked, "Are you OK? Did you hurt yourself? What happened?" I asked about 10 questions before he could answer. He looked at me and answered rather quickly and said, "No Mom, I did not hurt myself". "Are you sure?" He said,

"Yes Momma." "Ok, but what happened?"

This time I gave him a chance to answer. He

replied, "I fell at band practice." That's when my

mothering instinct kicked in. I had to make him

feel better and somehow take away that

embarrassing feeling. I proceeded to remind

him of a similar situation I had experienced. By

no means am I an expert on child rearing, but I

really thought my story would ease his pain.

Reflecting on one of my most embarrassing

days, I reminded him of the day I was at an

exercise camp and we had to run almost like a

relay and tag your partner and run back. Well,

somehow my first run resulted in me falling

face-first. Yes, really embarrassing but I dusted myself off, got up and continued to run to my partner. I tagged her, then proceeded to run back, and fell again. I fell going and coming. I thought nothing could more embarrassing that that. It was awful. Even a friend of mine said if it would have happened to her, she would have stopped and hid behind a tree. (I thought that was funny.) Surely, that story would show him everyone has embarrassing moments and survived. He looked at me with this blank stare as if to say, "Really Mom, it's not about you. *I* fell in band practice today!" As a mother of one, and I repeat, no expert I realized at that point, being a teenager means it's all about them.

* * *

Another day when I was picking up my son

from school, I was a little early before the

dismissal bell rang, so I parked and waited. As

my son approached the car, he got in and like

every day, I asked, "How was your day?" "Fine,"

he replied. With such busy congestion in the

parking lot, a parent politely gave me the OK to

back up onto the highway. I forgot what was at

an angle behind me in the middle of the

road...the school zone sign. The answer to the

question you are thinking is... *YES*. I backed into

the sign. This was every child's worst

nightmare. My son looked at me and said, "You

hit the sign!" in front of everybody. He

proceeded to melt down in his seat. If my teenage son could have made himself invisible, he would have at that moment. Could it get worse? As we were driving away, I could hear a text go off on his phone. One of his teenage friends said "I saw your mom hit that sign." (You cannot make these things up.) As a parent, I am worried that I damaged my car; the only thing my son thought is that this was the worst day of his life.

The moral to these stories is not how to embarrass your teenage son. These stories result from one of the changes I made in my life. I gave him the time I was giving my job. I feel so blessed to say is that I was there to be a part of these precious moments. No one had to tell me what happened. Certain memories stay with you forever. When you think about them, you relive them as if they just took place. These are moments in time when I felt what he felt, heard what he said, and tried to heal his "wounds". You try to be serious, and not to laugh because you are thinking, "This is such a small worry." But, this is not the time to share that with your son. That is living to me. Maybe not every day I can be there to pick him up from school. Maybe not every day I can experience what he is experiencing. I know I cannot be with him 24 hours a day, seven days a week.

Now, there is no more leaving to go to work before my son opens his eyes in the morning or coming home some days after he has closed his eyes to go sleep at night. I made that change. Now, I found a balance for me with work and being able to enjoy more time with my family as well. Every day I tell him I love him. I love our conversations. We pray together. We communicate the best we know how for a parent and teenager. I am so blessed to have him. My son is someone near and dear to my heart. He was a very important reason that I knew I had to make a change. Very soon, I will turn around again, and he will be graduating high school. He will be living his adult life and making his own journey.

(A note from my son, "Mom don't use my real name!")

Surely, this is not a book about regrets. It is about how I took charge of my life. I learned how to live for today. I cannot relive the past; time I missed with my family I cannot get back, but I can enjoy and make memories in the present.

It's only natural for us to look back and want to change the past. We grieve for the loss of time with loved ones, family, and friends. There are things we wish we had done and said, or not. But, God gives us mercy, and forgiveness. Forgiving ourselves of the past can be one of the hardest things. We must use our newly-

changed heart to learn to live a better life.

Testimony of Goodness, Mercy and Grace

Psalm 124:1 *If the Lord had not been on our side...*

There is not a day that goes by that I don't acknowledge

God for His mercy and grace. Fifteen years ago my life

changed at a level that words cannot express. God chose

to take my husband home to glory. It was during those

trying years that I had to trust God.   I had to learn

through God's Word to lean and depend on Him. You

see I had depended on my husband for EVERYTHING!

Isaiah 54:5 *For your Maker is your husband, the Lord*

Almighty is his name. I didn't respect nor understand

that *my* husband was the head of my life. He took care

and provided for me. He protected me.   Just as Christ is

the head of the Church. Ephesians 5:25 *Husbands, love*

your wives, as Christ loved the church and gave himself

up for her. (KJV) It's still difficult to say because when I

search deep, I realize that I used his kindness and desire

to please me in whatever way possible. When he tried

to provide me guidance and wise counsel it was nothing for me to let him know that I worked and I made decisions on what I wanted but not with his input. I remember one day when he looked at me at a loss for words because I bought a high- ticket item that definitely was not a necessity. I didn't realize until his death that he had stopped advising me because I was resistant to counsel . This is where my eyes were opened after his death, when I looked at the mountain of debt that I had to contend with because I didn't listen to my husband nor seek God's Word in regards to what Proverbs 31 describes as the woman with wisdom. If I had an additional day or hour in time could I have stopped to listen to God's Word? Or would I not take the time to tell my husband how much I loved and appreciated all he had done and was doing for me and our kids? Why did I not go to God's Word at that time to seek His Word as to how the wife should honor the head of her home?

The awesome testimony is how God's grace is always abounding. He spoke loudly to me in the years following my husband's death. The experience I endured, God has never removed His hands. He's opened my eyes to the order set forth in His Word- Christ is the Head of the Church and the ministry is set forth to guide the body of Christ as man is the head of his house. A man that prays and serves God in spirit and truth is an honor and the wife and children must fall under that order. I thank God that He did open my eyes to follow His Word and His Word will sustain me. He is a forgiving and merciful God and is all-knowing! If I had an additional hour I would stop and admire the things of God, stop and tell friends and loved ones how much I appreciate them being in my life and accepting me for who I am, for encouraging and pushing me when I feel like giving up. If I had another hour in time that dated back to fifteen years ago, I would say to my husband I respect your ideas and would listen to his words of warning not allowing me to have those fleshly desires and with him seek God in prayer. With the assistance of the Holy Ghost, we should have waited on God. God did not provide that additional hour in time with my husband but He has given me the opportunity to share with others to follow God's roadmap. He will never leave you nor forsake you.

Proverbs 31:10-31(KJV)

Who can find a virtuous woman? for her price is far above rubies. The heart of her husband doth safely trust in her, so that he shall have no need of spoil. She will do him good and not evil all the days of her life. She seeketh wool, and flax, and worketh willingly with her hands. She is like the merchants' ships; she bringeth her food from afar. She riseth also while it is yet night, and giveth meat to her household, and a portion to her maidens. She considereth a field, and buyeth it: with the fruit of her

hands she planteth a vineyard. She girdeth her loins with

strength, and strengtheneth her arms. She perceiveth

that her merchandise is good: her candle goeth not out by

night. She layeth her hands to the spindle, and her hands

hold the distaff. She stretcheth out her hand to the poor;

yea, she reacheth forth her hands to the needy. She is not

afraid of the snow for her household: for all her

household are clothed with scarlet. She maketh herself

coverings of tapestry; her clothing is silk and purple. Her

husband is known in the gates, when he sitteth among the

elders of the land. She maketh fine linen, and selleth it ;

and delivereth girdles unto the merchant. Strength and

honour are her clothing; and she shall rejoice in time to

come. She openeth her mouth with wisdom; and in her

tongue is the law of kindness. She looketh well to the

ways of her household, and eateth not the bread of

idleness. Her children arise up, and call her blessed; her husband also, and he praiseth her. Many daughters have done virtuously, but thou excellest them all. Favour is deceitful, and beauty is vain: but a woman that feareth the Lord, she shall be praised. Give her of the fruit of her hands; and let her own works praise her in the gates.

Anonymous

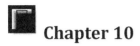 **Chapter 10**

Mind, Body, and Spirit

The Mind

A true relationship with the mind, body, and spirit will help you to connect with what is really important in your life.

Roman 8:6 *The mind governed by the flesh is death, but the mind governed by the Spirit is life and peace.*

What a profound scripture. To focus on the external is death, while focusing on the internal is the gateway to life and peace.

We must rid our mind of the noise that speaks to us from the world. Do not let earthly circumstances dictate our feelings or behaviors. We need to focus our thoughts on Him.

Romans 12:2 *Do not conform to the pattern of this world, but be transformed by the renewing of your mind. Then you will be able to test and approve what God's will is- His good ,pleasing and perfect will.* Do not allow the negative thoughts to take hold of your positive thoughts. Renew your mind by patiently waiting and trusting in God's word. Allow God to direct your path.

My revelation came when my son asked me a question. I knew at that point how far I had come in the renewing of my mind and thought process. He said, "Mom, what three words describe you on a good day?" After a minute or two of consideration, I answered with these three words: *"Blessed, grateful, and humbled."*

Then he asked me for three words that describe me on a bad day. Again, with careful thought, I answered: *"Blessed, grateful, and humbled."*

I explained to him that I did not always feel that way. There were many times when I felt the world made me who I am. We are all born into different circumstances, but it is about choices we make. Sometimes we make good choices, sometimes not so good choices. We choose to go right when we should have gone left. A lot of the time we try to take the easy way out, instead of taking time to do the right thing. Our pathways are not always smooth. It is good to take the road less traveled because it gives an opportunity to see and take in new things. There is always a lesson in the journey. We should use that lesson and learn to make better choices in life and improve our lives. It is always a thought process. I did not wake up one morning to that conclusion. It transpired over time.

I am so blessed for what God did not allow to happen to me over my years. For there were times when I did not make the right choices in my life, but now I could see how God stepped in and used people to direct me. I am blessed because of what He *did* allow, because my trials brought about change, strength, growth and a testimony. I am blessed because I see through opened eyes how far I have come in my life. I am blessed to have my family around me. I am more blessed than I deserve.

I am grateful because of all that I have! I know God gave me all that I have and in a blink of an eye, it can be taken away. I never try to take anything for granted. I am grateful for God's forgiveness, when I did not trust Him and put my trust in man. When I did not thank Him enough or fell short of giving Him all the praise, He still loved me more than I could love myself.

I am grateful that He continues to keep me. He provides guidance for me to live through His word.

I am humbled because every day is a learning experience for me. It teaches me the ways of life are not always fair, but I know that God is in control. He is always there to protect me. And I am so thankful.

We all do experience not -so-good days when we may feel a wide variety of emotions from anger to sadness on a daily basis. Whatever or whomever may have triggered those feeling to manifest, the flesh will react. We are only human. But we cannot allow that negativity to consume our thoughts because at end of the day, we must find that inner voice that lets us know we are the same beautiful people that God created us to be. We must know that we are still blessed, grateful, and His humbled servant. A plan is constructed for us by God to build and mold us to make us who we are but along the way there will be ups and downs. Jeremiah 29:11 "*For I know the plans I have for you," declares the Lord, "plans to prosper you and not harm you, plans to give you hope and a future.*"

Testimony of Insight

Part 2 continued from chapter 4 (Testimony of Growth).

Hi, this is Ashley again. Well, the plan God has for me has been quite a ride now.. but it all worked out for the better! He never left me down and He never will. Well that was through the teenage years I was speaking about earlier... that kind of lifestyle does not change overnight. I quit high school because I missed so many days in the 12th grade. I completed high school, with my GED. Even a 3.8 average could not keep me in school. I remember people telling me I ought to be ashamed of myself. They had not seen a score like that in a long time. I surely had the knowledge! It's a shame I let the world slip me away from myself.

Still, trying to find myself, I acted a fool. There were periods of legal troubles that lead to jail time and probation. I am now working, doing everything I can to stay focused. I am so dedicated to my new job that after five months I am already in line to be an assistant manager! I have been pulling extra hours and days for whoever needed me... but still had all those so-called friends.

After working another double shift and closing that night, I was invited over to a friend's house for a home cooked meal. Leaving to return home, around 12:30-1 o'clock in on a Tuesday morning is when it happened. I must have fallen asleep at the wheel. I was probably in and out of sleep at the stoplight waiting! When I noticed the light turn green, I proceeded to drive thinking I was turning onto an intersection. I did not realize that I was about 20 feet before the stoplight and that right turn caused me to have an accident that left me in a coma. Fortunately, I did not hit anyone. All I know is God had this all planned out for a reason! I had to almost die , to see how precious life really is. Maybe,

He saw that I still had not been on the right track, falling into other circumstances. Who knows? Seven years later, I've became a whole different person but I am still the fun-loving person I always was in life. I just now have a different outlook of what is fun.

I placed myself in rehab to right all the wrongs I had done in life. I found a church home. I know He carried me through this ordeal with a positive loving family . It's like He orchestrated every movement for the better. He knew I couldn't do this thing called life on my own down the road. Praise be unto Him! I am giving thanks to the One who truly deserves it!

Ashley

The Body

1 Corinthians 6:19 *Do you not know that your bodies are temples of the Holy Spirit, who is in you, whom you have received from God? You are not your own.*

Treat your body like the temple it was meant to be. This is your resting place. Do not abuse it with stress, hurt, harm and dangers.

I neglected my body by putting too much stress upon myself. We all have different stressors in life. They can vary from work, family, financial or health or a combination. Too many times, we are put under pressure to get the job done. Too many physical and physiological problems stem from stress. When we are stressed the following may happen to our bodies:

Our blood pressure may rise causing our heart to be used more to keep that blood pumping. This could bring stress to that muscle.

Our digestive system slows down which may result in decreased appetite and weight loss or weight gain.

Our heart rate(pulse) rises causing the heart to beat faster, again, bringing stress onto the muscle.

Our immune system may decrease and our body's defense system is weakened causing us not to be able to fight off disease.

Our muscles may become tense. We feel like we cannot relax.

We do not sleep (heightened state of alertness) which causes less rest. Getting three, maybe four hours a night of sleep may cause us to awake with that tired feeling we carry with us all day.

How our body responds to the stress affects our health. We have a "fight or flight" response in our body's sympathetic nervous system. This is the part of our system that is responsible for helping to regulate some of our main body functions such as heart rate and breathing. What that means is that our body goes into survival mode and the body will do anything to survive in the situation given.

While we are busy getting the job done, we are not seeing that the stress we are putting on our bodies can be very harmful.

Our nutritional health plays a very important role in keeping our body strong. With stress, sometimes we succumb to bad eating habits. Just like an automobile which needs gas to run on, our body needs food for fuel. Just like the car, our body is accustomed to a particular kind of fuel. Too many empty calories and not enough good things to fill our tanks will cause us to run slow.

Stress and anxiety can cause muscle tension as I previously stated. We must learn to allow our muscles to relax and that includes our heart muscle. We are slowly breaking down our temple, one brick at a time. You may not see the effects today or tomorrow but just like with any structure, slowly the brick and mortar will crumble. We are only as strong as the weakest link in the chain. Once that link is broken, the destruction process has started. I want to say I had all the above or I felt like it. I was consistently tired and no matter how hard I tried there is no such thing as 'catching up on sleep'. I could not concentrate or focus on one particular thing. My mind was a clutter of disorder.

Can we stop it?

I did! I had to stop the long hours of work. No amount of money was worth it, if I could not live to see and enjoy its benefits. I had to increase my sleeping hours. No more three and four hours of sleep at night. I had to give my body time to recover from all the noise of the day. I made time in my new plan to give rest to my temple. I removed some of the stressors or stimuli that caused stress in my life. I had to change my old habits that were wearing me down, and start new ones to build me up. My new job consisted of working to fill my temple with positive energy and better nutritional habits. I was making the effort to eat healthier and not skipping meals to try to gain that extra hour. I started an exercise program to make my temple stronger to build up my endurance for my long venture ahead. My best was yet to come. I had to be ready. Take a look at what is best for you and what can work for you to get your temple ready.

Testimony of Healing

As the Bible says in Philippians 4:13 *I can do all things through Christ which strengthens me.*

In March of the year of our Lord and Savior Jesus Christ twenty eleven(2011), I was proceeding to do my task of meditating and studying every Saturday before preaching God's word to His people on Sunday's service. I am the pastor of two churches.

A close friend of mine called and asked what was my schedule for that morning knowing I was studying a sermon. He asked could I come and help him cut a limb down off a tall pine tree. I said yes as I need to get back to my assignment of being prepared to serve God's people.

When I got there about a half hour from my home, I told him let me go up and cut the limb down as I was three years younger than he was. We had cut many trees down for many people. I noticed something the Holy Spirit allowed me to see; large ants crawling along side the tree.

They were carpenter ants. I had heard about but never seen them. I knew they could eat the inside of a tree or it's limb, leaving the outside looking unharmed. I climbed the ladder about 25-30 feet. After being unconscious for minutes I noticed that I was in an emergency vehicle headed to the hospital. The EMS personnel informed me that I had fallen a great height and I was on route to the hospital.

I went through many tests and examinations and was discharged from the hospital with a sprain on my left arm, and medication was given to me. There was no noticeable harm done other than sore muscles and stiffness. In a month's time it was noticed by my wife

Patricia that I was moving slower than I used to, leaning sideward, slow in speech, and there was a change in my attitude. After being diagnosed by my primary doctor with a change in my equilibrium, I continued to my normal routines.

The following Thursday, I drove to a church I pastor 72 miles from my home. I was involved in Bible class that evening , and after service someone notice that I was acting strangely.

After leaving Bible study, I left and drove south in the opposite direction of my home Baton Rouge, Louisiana where I live. An associate minister from the church telephoned my wife and informed her that he had seen me turning in the opposite direction of traveling back home. After I circled around my old high school I finally parked and my associate minister drove me back to Baton Rouge.

I was still unaware of my surroundings. Patricia decided that it was time to go to the hospital directed by the Holy Spirit. She and my younger son brought me to the emergency room. My older son was right behind them.

I was diagnosed with a subdural hematoma. I had bleeding on the brain from the fall I had sustained. I needed surgery to relieve the increased pressure on the brain.

During my surgery, God showed me a place I had never seen before. I saw a beautiful forest of greenery, white and blue buildings and Mom and Dad looking ahead, but not at me. I remember saying, "Mom I'm sick but you're not looking at me." I saw a picture of my older brother's face. He was killed in the Vietnam war and I heard a voice saying in the background "NO! NO!"

My surgery lasted five hours.

After the surgery I was told by the surgeon that I kept saying a phrase before going to sleep, "If I have done all You want me to..."

I stayed in the ICU ward for seven days and another seven days in the hospital recovering from brain surgery with 64 staples. It was amazing to the doctors that my speech, activity, and mind was not affected. It was like nothing had happened.

God is the head of my life, He is my all in all. If it had not been for Him I cannot imagine what my life would be like. I thank Him every day for what He does for me and what He has brought me through. I thank Him for bringing me through the surgery and allowing my wife and sons to take care of me. I thank God for my daughters-in law and those beautiful grandchildren who put that big smile on my face. I thank all my family and friends who supported me when I needed them.

April 16th, 2016 was five years since the surgery. A year after the surgery I was back in the pulpit preaching and doing all the things I love doing. It was clear to me that God had other things He wanted me to do in this world. I know now the answer to the phrase continued to repeat "If I have done all You want me to..." He has shown me that He is not through with me yet.

My thought to all is *Finally, brethren, whatsoever things are true, whatsoever things are honest, whatsoever things are just, whatsoever things are pure, whatsoever things are lovely, whatsoever things are of good report; if there be any virtue, and if there be any praise, think on these things.* Philippians 4:8 (KJV)

With Thoughts and Prayers,
Rev. Charles Edward Harkless, Sr.

The Spirit

Galatians 5:22-23 *But the fruit of the Spirit is love, joy, peace, forbearance, kindness, goodness, faithfulness, gentleness and self-control. Against such things there is no law.*

Romans 15:13 *May the God of hope fill you with all joy and peace as you trust in him, so that you may overflow with hope by the power of the Holy Spirit.*

John 14:26 *But the Advocate, the Holy Spirit, whom the Father will send in my name, will teach you all things and will remind you of everything I have said to you.*

As we look at the scripture, the spirit encompasses all the fruit of our being. We receive direction, wisdom, knowledge and comfort through the power of the Holy Spirit. We are of the world, of the flesh, but an inner peace is found in the heart. It is a belief in a Godly spirit, a righteous spirit that brings truth, honor and peace to your life. Find that balance in your life. I found that relationship when I placed God first in my life. I don't know when it happened but my busyness had become a distraction to what was really important. God had become just a *part* of my life, and not the Head of my life. My spiritual life felt empty and I lacked the understanding to fill me. Through

Him again, I found the strength and courage to turn my life around.

Ephesians 3:20 *Now unto him that is able to do exceeding abundantly above all that we ask or think, according to the power that worketh in us.*

The changes were not easy to make. Nor did they happen overnight. "Stress makes you believe that everything has to happen right now. Faith reassures you that everything will happen in God's timing." Author unknown. I placed my faith in God to allow me to do all that needed to be done.

In Psalm 73:26 *My flesh and my heart may fail,*

but God is the strength of my heart and my

portion forever.

Testimony of a Spiritual Awakening

I have always considered myself a Christian. I was baptized as a baby into the church and later confirmed that faith by embracing Christianity in the Sacrament of Confirmation. Being brought up Catholic, I received all the Sacraments according to the laws of the Catholic Church. As I became a young adult, my faith suffered because although I was attending weekly Mass, I found myself just going through the motions. I was existing and living my life according to me. I was reaching my goals. I went to college, got married, had children and started my career. All were my plans. I never thought of living according to God's plan. As a matter of fact, I found myself pregnant before I was married. Therefore, because my husband was married previously in the Catholic Church, we weren't able to marry in the church without my husband getting an annulment. We had two children and have been married for 28 years. Life continued, and we raised our children as Catholics. We attended Sunday Mass with the children and went about our lives. I sat in church and thought about where we were going to eat after, or what I had to do after Mass. I never gave the meaning of Mass a second thought. Life passed me by and it passed by fast! Up until a few years ago, I thought being a Christian was simply going to church on Sunday. My faith really started coming alive with the death of my father to cancer in 2008. It was then that I realized that life was passing us all. I always thought that I had time to get right with God. I was young and healthy! I wasn't going to die any time soon. I realized that I had taken so much for granted. God was in control. I was only existing, not living! I began to develop my faith by simply doing the only thing I knew to do, and that was to pray. I started a habit of praying the rosary every morning. The more I continued that habit the more my faith grew and the stronger my relationship with God. I no longer took life for granted. I saw every day as a blessing and a gift. I felt an uncontrollable desire to learn more about my faith and about growing closer to Jesus. I wanted more than anything else to please God and to do His will. I felt the presence of the Holy Spirit like never before. My weekly Sunday Mass experience became really intense, the homilies on Sundays always seemed to be just what I needed to hear. It was as if God was talking directly to me!! As my faith grew, the fact that I wasn't married in the church really began to bother me. I went back to confession after 20 years. The more I would talk to the priest the more I could feel God leading me to what He wanted me to do. After many prayers and meditations and listening to God speak to me, my husband and I renewed our vows and were married in the church. We made a covenant with God to put Him in the center of our marriage. Even though may husband's first marriage had been annulled, it was not until 27 years later, we decided to get our marriage blessed. Mark 10:6-8 (NKJV) *But from the beginning of creation, 'God made them male and female. For this reason a man shall leave his father and mother and be joined to his wife, and the two shall become one flesh. So then they are no longer two but one flesh.* I know this was nothing but divine intervention. We never even talked about it anymore. I know that the voice inside me leading me to this was the voice of my Savior. He was now in control of my life. He was answering prayers. He was moving mountains and doing things in my life that I never thought would happen. My marriage is stronger than it has ever been. My husband and I make it a point **to pray together** before bed every night. Hebrews 11:1 Faith is *the realization of what is hoped for and evidence of things not seen.* I had a void that I filled up with Jesus. I could definitely feel His presence in my life. Whether it is in a song, a daily scripture verse, my daily rosary or a voice from a coworker and friend, God speaks to us. I now pray about everything. I gave everything to God. I thank Him daily for the blessings He gives me and my family. I am even stepping way out of my comfort zone by teaching religion classes at my parish church. I started going to weekly adoration. This is where I sit in front the Body of Christ and reflex and worship Him In His Real Presence. I joined a Bible study group. I felt such a strong calling.

Recently diagnosed with endometrial cancer, I know now that God was preparing me all along for my cross. This is my chance to share in my Savior's suffering. How blessed am I to be able to carry my cross! If I hadn't answered God's call, I know that I would not have the courage and bravery to carry my cross. He wants us to turn to Him for all our struggles, trials, fears and anxiety, and He will show us His plans for each of us. Only through our sufferings are we humbled and able to enter the Kingdom of God. It is through His love for us that we will be victorious over evil. Mark 11:24 *Therefore I tell you, all that you ask for in prayer, believe that you will receive it and it shall be yours.* Sometimes God uses us to fulfill our own prayers. We become his instrument. Through these trials and my suffering, I have come to know Jesus. He used my father's death and my cancer diagnosis to strengthen my faith. My relationships with others have grown and strengthened as well. All aspects of my life have grown, and I can see God's love in my husband, my coworkers, my family and my children. It so easy now to live out my life and God's plan for me. My marriage is stronger than it has ever been. We both are growing in faith together instead of individually. Philemon 1:6 *I pray that you may be active in sharing your faith, so that you will have a full understanding of every good thing we have in Christ.* We are all called by name. We need to take time to listen to His call. We are called to serve God. Faith without service will lead to death. We need to grow constantly in our relationship with God because we are called to be disciples. I was dead in my faith, and I went through the motions of life. By responding to the call, I am able to live my life according to the Lord's plan. I feel more joy and happiness. I even feel more energetic and physically fit. Without the crosses and pain in my life, I would still be lost. Therefore, rejoice when given the opportunity to share in our Lord's suffering. It is the way to God's Kingdom and eternal happiness. Now is the time!

R.D.

 **Chapter 11**

Do Something Positive That is Out of Your Comfort Zone.

A comfort zone is a beautiful place, but nothing ever grows there.-Unknown

Do not become complacent in where you are in your life. I lived in constant motion and was getting nowhere, because I became satisfied with my life and did nothing to make it better. I now realize where there is growth, there is learning. Where there is growth, there is *change.* Where there is growth, there is *awareness.* Where there is growth, there is *life.*

Where there is growth, there is *strength*. Where there is growth, there is *healing*. I needed to step out of my comfort zone.

Encouraged by a friend to start an exercise program, my thoughts were, "I can do that." Then she told me it would be outdoors and involve running. First, she lost me with outdoors. I am not an "outside, look at nature" kind of person. Inside a gym, out of the rain, out of the heat, and air-conditioned would be the better option. Running and outdoors was not. My change is still in progress. You can't just have faith, you need to walk the walk and not just talk the talk.

James 2:17 *Even so faith, if it hath not works, is dead, being alone. (KJV)*

The first day of class, we were tested on our endurance level before we started the program. This included timed sit-ups, pushups and I had to run/jog a mile. Way out of my comfort zone. Never had I run since high school, and even then I was still out of my comfort zone.

Never the less, I took the test and made the mile with a combination of walking, jogging, and running. (Maybe not in that order). I survived and my total time was not bad for a first time.

Everybody in the group was so very supportive. They encouraged me to come back and I was so motivated by the results, I decided to go back.

And I did, again, again, and again. I loved it The

environment was so positive . In fact, I set a goal

for myself to run that mile in my record time

just for me. I became a advocate for the fit-

camp. It was not only a way to get my body

(temple) back in shape and feel healthier, it

gave me a way to relieve the stressors of the

day. I was so focused on that hour of fit-training,

it provided me with an avenue to relax my

mind. As a result of the program, I gained more

confidence to do things I thought I could not do

before. It improved my mood, I felt better

physically and mentally.   I was introduced to

great people of all ages with such positive

outlooks. They had such a winning spirit. But we need to listen to bodies; all exercise is not for everyone. Look at what is good for you. We will never know what we are missing if we never try to step out our comfort zone.

Blessed are friends who encourage you and stand by you in helping you to make a positive change.

***

Isaiah 6:8 *Then I heard the voice of the Lord saying, "Whom shall I send? And who will go for us?" And I said, "Here am I. Send me!"*

As promised, here is my story about my travels to Tennessee. As stated before, I know God places people in your life for a reason. He continues to use us as His vessels to reach the broken and the suffering. Still searching for purpose and at a pivotal time in my life when I felt that all the burdens I tried to bear were weighing me down, I did not know my next step. I received a spiritual connection with this man of God who had a ministry that spoke to me and a testimony that was anointing. As I followed his ministry, it left me with a desire to get closer to God and seek His word. I wanted to give back and be of service and do God's will. Fast forward, less than a year later, I connected with my spiritual brother by way of telephone. It was nothing but God that made this happen. In our conversation, he invited me to be part of a Recovery Festival which was a vision of his that celebrated men and women that are recovering in their trials and witness their strong determination.   I said yes to the call.

As I hung up the phone, I shared with my husband my testimony. Then I began to doubt that I could do the job. *"Me!?" "Why not you? replied my husband." I am no public speaker. No one knows me, I said"* "You were called because of what you do and your gift" as I was reminded by my husband. God uses everyone for His purpose.

 In 2014, the month of September, my husband and I traveled from a small town in Louisiana to Nashville, Tennessee. As I realize, no distance was too far when you are doing God's work. Being a nurse by profession, my assignment was to answer questions and educate on the disease of addiction from a medical aspect for the Recovery Festival. My husband and I stayed for three days and were blessed by anointing testimonies, fellowship, and powerful praise and worship services. Who but God could make this happen? I now know that there are no coincidences. People are brought together for His greater good. With a grateful heart, I received this opportunity, and stepped out on faith. I prepared myself, armed with a wealth of information to share. I did all my research. Who knew years later that I would return to my roots as a nurse working in the field of substance abuse? God was preparing me way back then. I dedicated myself to the cause. I stood in front of an unknown audience with a microphone and notes in hand, and I allowed God to use me. With all this worldly preparation, I needed to be prepared spiritually. This scripture spoke to me:

Isaiah 55:11 *So shall my word be that goeth forth out of my mouth: it shall not return unto me void, but it shall accomplish that which I please, and it shall prosper in the thing whereto I sent it.*

I knew in my heart God would give me the words I needed to say. And all was well. If I helped one person make a difference in their life for the good, I did what I set out to do. I was able to give back to the community my gift of nursing through teaching and educating. This was such a rewarding and humbling experience. This blessing opened a door for me to be of service for what God had called me to do. It was nothing short of amazing to meet and greet people whose lives were changed through their testimonies and realness. This experience also brought me closer to God's Word and I learned to trust that you should never be afraid to step out of your comfort zone, because He can turn your impossible into possible. Even after the door was opened, I continued my education and became a substance abuse practitioner because I knew God had more plans for me. He

gave me a purpose.

Testimony of Choice

My name is Denise and I was born and raised in Louisiana.

Out of five siblings (two boys and three girls) I was the only one that was very shy. Yes, I was the one that held on to my little sister's coattail.

At a young age, I always thought there was something special about me, but not really knowing what that special was. Crazy isn't it? I just knew.

I was raised by my mother, a single parent, who became a widow at a young age. Everything was not at its best at times, but my mother whom I admire dearly, did everything she could to make sure we were well taken care of. Because I was shy, everyone around me expected I would be the one that would turn out OK.

At the age of eight, an elder friend of the family whispered to me that the man that I thought was my father was not my biological father. For seven years I kept that secret. I was scared and confused. Even though I didn't know God, I felt His presence with me at times when I felt alone. Psalm 68:5 *A father of the fatherless, and a judge of the widows, is God in his holy habitation.*

At age 15, I met my biological father for the first time. I felt relief. Also at that age, I did not make the best decisions. I became pregnant at the age of 15 and had a beautiful baby girl. Now, as a teenage mother, there was one decision or choice I had to make. Should I drop out of high school in order to take care of my little girl? It was one of toughest decisions to have to make. But, little that I knew God had me on His mind . You see when we think all things seem to go wrong, He will cause them to work out for His good. At the age of 17, my daughter's father invited me to a Bible study that he attended on Friday nights.

I took him up on his invite and went to the Bible study. After that night, my life would never be the same. I was introduced to Jesus Christ as my Savior. I was born again, healed and set free. He has been so good to me. Jeremiah 29:11 says, *For I know the thoughts I have toward you says The Lord, thoughts of peace, and not of evil, to give you an expected end.* We do not always make the best decisions or choices in our lives, but God in his mercy and grace helps us along the way even when we don't know or realize He's there with us keeping and protecting us from harm's way.

 John 6:44 *No one can come to me unless the father who sent me draws him and I will raise him up.* I believe that God draws us to Him because of His love for us. As my relationship with God became stronger though prayer, worship and reading my Bible, there was nothing I could not do.

My vision in life became clearer. As I served God, He

began putting me in places that I couldn't even have imagined.   He has been teaching and educating me not only by the Holy Spirit but by mighty men and women of God that are in my life.

And, it all began at that small Bible study. Oh my how good is our God. I have been married to my little girl's biological father Graylin Thomas for now thirty-five years. We had four more beautiful children plus a niece we raised. All the children have graduated from high school and as for my baby, she graduated from college. My husband and I are pastors of New Harvest Church. God can do anything with someone who gives Him their whole heart. I turned out OK.

God Bless, Denise Thomas

 **Chapter 12**

Finding Purpose

As defined by Merriam-Webster, purpose is "the reason why something is done or used: the aim or intention of something."

God gives us purpose. We are predestined to walk in His plan. For too long I lived a busy life. I continued on that same path that *I* had set for myself. I knew something was missing in my life but could not fill that void. I thought the answer was to be more busy to replace that empty feeling. I gave myself more work to do, more jobs to finish, and carried other people's burdens. Little did I know it was only a distraction to what God had planned for me. He gives you free will to make choices. Unfortunately my choices lead to confusion and chaos.

What was my destiny that God had planned for me? I did not know. As I continued to fill every waking minute with "purpose" as defined in Webster's dictionary, I realize later that "purpose" meant so much more. It was more than completing all the chores. It was more than my job. Purpose was more than setting a goal and moving on to the next one. According to Proverbs 16:9 *In their hearts humans plan their course, but the Lord establishes their steps.*

Our steps are ordered by the Lord. Our trials, our choices, our journey, our testimony make up our purpose. Every individual has their own test and trial to go through. Through our test we make choices, and from those choices our journey is created. From our journey we are a living testimony to what God can do and bring us through when you trust Him.

When we try to fulfill our own destiny without God's help, we continue to live in confusion and not peace. I was seeking peace of mind without God's help. As I continued to exist and not live the life that He intended for me to live, I continued to feel empty. I needed to be filled with His purpose. I needed a reason to wake up

every morning. I needed a purpose that was
everlasting. I needed a spiritual healing.

As I read in Romans 8:28 *And we know that in
all things God works for the good of those who
love Him, who have been called according to His
purpose.*

I know that my trials are meant for me to learn
and reflect, but God continues to guide me and
in the end it will work out for my good.

My purpose is to serve Him and glorify Him. I
found a way to use my gift of caring and my
compassion to walk in purpose. My profession
as a nurse was the catalyst that enabled me to
move forward and fill that void. I want to be

able to help others live the best life. I want to

be a blessing, not a burden. I felt my calling was

to be of service and teach His people. We all

have different purposes in life. You have to find

what fills your heart with joy, find that

something that brings passion in your life. You

will know because when you talk about it, it

will bring a smile to your face. Many have told

me when I talk about my purpose, they see joy.

When I needed a reason to keep going, when my

mind and body wanted to give up, that is when

my inner spirit gave me the strength to keep

going. Do not miss what God has planned for

you if you are still searching for that extra hour.

Whatever He has in store for you, God will give you the *time.*

Job 42:2 *I know that you can do all things; no purpose of yours can be thwarted.*

Testimony of Purpose

The Call to Ministry

I define a divine call as being the act of God calling someone on earth to do something that He has ordained for their life. I was an ordained Deacon at my father's church at the time of my calling and also served as the church's Adult Bible Study teacher and assistant Sunday School teacher. Those duties within the church actually brought me closer to God and His Word in themselves. My earthly father is my pastor and he has inspired me to follow God's lead in the path He has for my life.

As a young minister, I have learned quickly one thing that preachers get asked all the time. That question is, "How do you know you were called?" My calling was a very unique experience. For that past year 2013 –2014, I had been feeling like I was called because of the many dreams I was having where it seemed like I was always running from something or someone. But what was chasing me never revealed itself. On May 5, 2014, I delivered a message at church and felt something spiritual that I had never felt before. On that fifth day of the fifth month, God allowed me to deliver a message from the fifth chapter of John about the man at the pool of Bethesda which had five porches. I told myself God was trying to tell me something because he wanted me to deliver that message on that day. The way things lined up with that number five was no coincidence. There was something about that number five.

So I continued to pray to the Lord because I wondered if God had called me to the ministry on that day. And I prayed and asked God to show me if that was true. God used my middle daughter to show me. A few days later that week, I brought her to the dentist. It's truly amazing because she was five years old at the time. The dentist said she had five cavities that needed to be filled. Two weeks later, I brought her to the doctor for some neck pain. They weighed her on the scale. She weighed 55.5 pounds. God allowed me to graduate from seminary college in the fifth month of 2014. The number five spiritually is the number of grace. Grace is a five-letter word. It is something about that number five because God's grace allowed me to deliver my first sermon on a fifth Sunday of the month.

I am truly convinced of God's calling.

It was something that I had prayed about and relied on three voices to verify this calling:

1. The voice of God

2. The voice of a Pastor

3. My own voice

The Lord has truly made a difference in my life, from my true conversion experience to my calling to the ministry. I have accepted this call and look forward to continue doing what God has called me to do!

Minister Charles E. Harkless, Jr.

 **Chapter 13**

Take a Day and Do Nothing

A quote from British philosopher, historian, and writer Bertrand William (1872-1970)is " The time you enjoy wasting is not wasted time."

What happens if I do nothing today? The world will not stop revolving on its axis. The sun will still rise in the east and still set in the west.

* * *

I would like for you to participate in an exercise with me... Stop whatever you are doing right now if you can. Relax and take a couple of deep breaths. Release all that tension that you have been carrying. From the top of your head to the soles of your feet, let it go. This is your time. There is no stress, no chaos, and no confusion. Clear your mind of any negative thoughts and focus on yourself. Take a look at everything positive in your life. Embrace your moment. You are right here, right now. Take a minute to count your many blessings. Make sure to include yourself, because you are a blessing, a blessing to your friends and family, your job, and the people you meet. I want you to end this exercise by speaking a positive word over your life because we know that *Death and life are in the power of the tongue, and those who love it will eat its fruit.* Proverbs 18:21

Practice doing this simple exercise every day. You will be amazed at the positive results.

* * *

We are not slaves to the outside world with all the hustle and bustle of the highways and by-ways. We can receive a day where there is no traffic. Free yourself from the noise. Just let go and let God. *Cast your cares on the* Lord and *He will sustain you; He will never let the righteous be shaken.* Psalm 55:22

Let the phone ring. If it's not God, your children, or the people closest to you calling, please ask them to leave a message. Too much of anything can become overwhelming. A lot of time we are talking to people and really not hearing a word they are saying because our minds are elsewhere.

Can we let the chores wait? It's OK if your bed is not made today. It's OK if that dish in the sink is not washed today. It's OK if you did not vacuum today. Really, how many times you have heard people say, "I took the day off". Now it's your turn to take a break from the clean up.

Take a social media break. I know it can be hard. Social media can be very entertaining. It can also be a diversion from our own struggles. It takes us away from our own life as we focus on others. We can even enjoy a funny post every now and then. We love the encouraging and positive words. But, for today, focus on your life and your needs.

Clear your mind of the day's clutter. Stop carrying all that baggage with you, everywhere you go. Keep all the good stuff, and remove all the not so good stuff. Recall the exercise in which we took a minute to relax. The baggage is the stress, tension, and negative thoughts. Stop trying to make room for things you don't need. Your mind is like a closet. As much as we try and fill it with more and more stuff, it becomes so cluttered that we cannot tell the new from the old. We cannot enjoy our positive thoughts because the negative ones have became entangled. Free yourself.

Learn to say no, and don't look back. No is one of the hardest, two-letter words for us to say.   As a child, we remember the word having a negative connotation. You could not do this or that. You cannot have this or that. As we got older, we internalized that it is not a 'positive' word. Maybe it's that controlling personality some of us have. Saying no made you feel like you could not do something;   it could have made you feel vulnerable, less strong. Whatever our reasons, well *no* more! Because today *'no'* only means... I just need a little me time. No more, no less! At the end of the day, have NO regrets!

What if I am not ready for the change? To everything there is season, and a time to every purpose under the heaven. Ecclesiastes 3:1(KJV).

It's not your time, and it's OK. You first must be able to recognize that a change needs to be made in your life. Many will enjoy the world and all it has to offer and believe it (the world) gives us happiness. As we know, the world holds nothing eternal. As our external happiness fades, we then see that our real joy comes from within. The world did not give it to us, and the world cannot take it away. It is a continual battle between the internal self and the external world. Until we can discern what is truly important for us to be at peace, then change will not happen. But, your time is near. Let God lead you into your season. When you are ready to commit to change, you will

whatever the situation may be.

Testimony of Commitment

This weekend I met with a financial planner and listened to her spiel on what was necessary to have the income sufficient to provide for possible long-term care in the event these services are required. As I listened to her, I felt something within me saying," This is not what God wants from you right now". You know there's nothing wrong with planning for the future but I just didn't feel pulled toward that direction although I was excited to set up our initial meeting. The meeting ended without me making a commitment but I thanked her for challenging me to dig deeper into that aspect of my life. Now today is Sunday and after having a great time worshipping and praising the Lord, I shared this experience with my friend who stated she understood my response because what is important to me is not the material aspects of life but where am I going to spend eternity? Just as one prepares for the future naturally we need to spiritually prepare our hearts and minds to live for Christ. I need to check out what type of investments I have made in my prayer life, have I invested in committing time to serve others in His name, have I mediated on His Word on a daily basis? When looking at spiritual long term- care, do I have enough Word in me that a physical Bible is not needed because that Word is in my heart? When looking at retirement from my natural job will I have invested enough in God's Word and His people to dedicate my life to Him and continue to be an example to others? The Word reminds us in Psalm 8:4 *What is man, that thou art mindful of him? and the son of man, that thou visitest him?"* God valued man so much that He sent His Son as a sacrifice for our sins. The price on man's head is so high there is no monetary value that can be established. We are God's greatest creation and the ransom paid is an investment none of us can make so to

God be the glory for the things He has done! I'm not advocating for not doing what one has to do to get their personal business in order. God wants us to use wisdom and take care of those things also but first and foremost my goal is to take care of the things of God first and I know He will guide me with the natural.

But seek first His kingdom and His righteousness, and all these things will be given to you as well. Matthew 6:33

Anonymous

 Chapter 14

Words of Encouragement

<u>2</u> Timothy 1:7 *For the Spirit God gave us does not make us timid, but gives us power, love and self-discipline.*

Change is not easy. For some of us we get too complacent in our thoughts, our ways, our lives. We learn to accept what *is* instead of living the life that God intended for us to live. We want things to be easy, but we must realize life is hard. It's hard because we make it hard. We want what we want, when we want it. We are impatient. We are too prideful. We can be selfish at times. We try to control and manipulate our situations to suit our needs. We want the straight path, one with no curves. We want things to go our way, because that's what we plan. We want *our* will to be done.

But if we just lay down *our* will, and live according to *God's* will, we find a way not to just exist, but really start living our best lives.

Psalm 143:10 *Teach me to do thy will; for thou art my God: thy spirit is good; lead me into the land of uprightness. (KJV)*

I want more of Him and less of me. *He must become greater, I must become less.* John 3:30

We must humble ourselves and appreciate all God's works and show gratitude every day.

I faced my journey knowing that there will be obstacles along the way. These obstacles that included the external and internal. I was misguided by the enemy's false promises and my impatience to see things change right away. Every day was not my best day, but I kept the faith and trusted in His Word. I placed God first in my life and know everything else will follow. So, be of good courage, God is not through with you. Greater things are about to happen.

Let us not become weary in doing good, for at the proper time we will reap a harvest if we do not give up. Galatians 6:9

A change will happen, just you wait and see.

Every day is a new day.

Testimony of a New Day

I was so pressed and pulled on every side. I couldn't get no rest and couldn't see no end in sight. I needed God to pull me through someone to show me what to do. Tired of being blue. Circumstances filled my life with such regrets. And every time I'd turn around trying to get my feet back on the ground. Many tears I had to cry. Sometimes it felt like I could die. Somebody tell me why. You gave me hope. Lord You gave me joy. Right in the midst of the storm. When my life was broken and torn. You wiped away the pain. And my life will never be the same. I want to thank you Lord. Thank you for a brand new day. I can take the storm the rain, the hurt, the pain...

Despite all that the enemy had conjured up against my life, I prevailed. I spent fifteen years running from what God had planned for me. I lived most of my youth in and out of Juvenile Detention centers because I kept

185

getting into trouble. I was charged with armed robbery, behavior problems, and just a loss of self- control. At the age of 15, I was introduced into using cocaine. For years, I felt lonely, depressed, and strung out. I felt comfort in isolating myself for days at a time. My family did not know where I was, or what I was doing or if I was alive for months. Feeling frustrated and powerless against the drugs and alcohol, I was in and out of rehabilitation centers. I found myself relapsing because I was not getting clean for the right reasons. The worst of times were when I would wake to another day as the sun started to rise and realize how I wasted another night from my family. Trouble continued to follow, until one Sunday morning waking up in a police station, I found myself looking at being charged with vehicular homicide. At that point, I knew I had to stop running from reality and allow God to step in my life. I asked for a Bible and for eight days straight that Bible did not move from my side. I rededicated my life to God and asked Him for a strategy to get me out of this mess. *Accountability* was His answer. You must be accountable and submit to the Heavenly Father. I felt a whole lot of people had given up on me. The judicial system wanted to put me away. Nobody trusted me, nobody believed in me, but God held on to me. Just when I thought I would self-destruct, God stepped into my life. This is an amazing story of the power of God. He took away my desire for drugs and alcohol. Wherever you are in your life and whatever you are going through, God can change your situation.

I can look at people in the eye and know that no matter where they are in their life, God can make a difference, because *God is bigger than their circumstances. They defeated him by the blood of the Lamb and by their testimony; for they did not love their lives but laid them down for him.* Revelation 12:11(TLB)

You cannot show people your blessed side unless you reveal the your broken side. Ministry emerges from the journey. You need to show and tell how you have gotten to where you are now. Don't be ashamed of your story, but allow it to inspire instead.

Have a different perspective and start looking at all the struggles that you are going through as progress rather than setbacks. Use what originally had ill intent to advance you and teach you. *You intended to harm me, but God intended it for good to accomplish what is now being done, the saving of many lives.* Genesis 50:20

And we know that in all things God works for the good of those who love Him, who have been called according to His purpose. Romans 8:28

God Bless---Pastor Wess Morgan

CONCLUSION

In All We Do, Give Thanks

O give thanks unto the Lord, for he is good: for his mercy endures for ever . Let the redeemed of the Lord say so, whom he has redeemed from the hand of the enemy. Psalm 107:1-2(KJV)

Through our testimonies, surely if God did this for me, He can do it for you. Through our testimonies, we find a healing and where others find hope.   Through our testimonies, we share His amazing grace and mercy.   Through our testimonies, we show that we are human and we make mistakes.

The enemy takes many forms in our lives. In the testimonies we have read we saw the enemy can take on many faces from alcohol, drugs, guilt, shame, stress, anger, sin, pride, disease, to depression. All come to destroy and take away our peace, and fill us with destruction and make us destitute. *The thief comes only to steal and kill and destroy; I have come that they may have life, and have it to the full.* John 10:10

I saw where the goodness of my life was slipping away so I made a change for the better. I saw where busyness does not come without distractions and regret. Now I feel when circumstances become too overwhelming for me, I can step back and allow God to take control. Just when we think we have everything under control, the forces of nature step in. Like an open door, it comes right in. But we must stand firm in our faith. Yes, there will be trials and tribulations that we all face because we are in the world. How do you face your problems? Do you give them to God? Or do you try to handle them yourself? As we struggle to find a sense of peace in our lives, we struggle with life itself. There are many enemies we are up against; the external, meaning the emotional, the physical, people, places, things and the internal, meaning we struggle with the heart and spirit. While we want to make changes in our lives, we are struggling with how to make that change. We cannot be stagnant in our life because we will not grow in spirit and learn life's lessons. Mistakes made we will be doomed to make again unless we change. *If I only had 25 hours in a day*...no more because I have learned to recognize the warning signs of destruction.

But God is with you in your battle. He said in Deuteronomy 31:6 *Be strong and of a good courage, fear not, nor be afraid of them: for the Lord thy God, he it is that doth go with thee; he will not fail thee, nor forsake thee.* (KJV)

In the testimonies, we saw the battles won: Not without bruises and scars. Not without regrets.

Not without shame and guilt. Not without pain and suffering, but won.

For the Lord your God is the one who goes with you to fight *for you against your enemies to give you victory.* Deuteronomy 20:4 (ESV)

The battle is not yours, it is the Lord's.

My prayer to you is that through my story and the testimonies of others, you will find what you need to make a change in your life, no matter how large or small the change. Through our trials, our strength comes. Through living, our joy is received. My prayer to you is to find spiritual direction. For once we discern what is important, change can happen.

Prayer of Discernment

"Heavenly Father, I want to live a life of no confusion. Help me to remove the chaos that has caused destruction, distraction, and disturbance in my life. Give me the wisdom and the knowledge to tell the difference between good and bad, right and wrong. Redirect my footsteps, if they are not Your steps. Give me the insight to discern what is clouded in darkness. Allow me to see what the naked eye cannot see. Allow me to hear what the natural ear cannot hear, so I may make wise choices. If I should stumble in the ways of man, I know You will not let me fall. I am asking this prayer in Jesus' Name.

Amen.

Proverbs 3:13-14 *Blessed is the one who finds wisdom, and the one who gets understanding, for the gain from her is better than the gain from silver and her profit better than gold.*

Prayer for Guidance in the Midst of

Perplexity

Psalm 143 1-12 (KJV)

Hear my prayer, O LORD, give ear to my supplications: in thy faithfulness answer me, and in thy righteousness.

And enter not into judgment with thy servant: for in thy sight shall no man living be justified.

For the enemy hath persecuted my soul; he hath smitten my life down to the ground; he hath made me to dwell in darkness, as those that have been long dead.

Therefore is my spirit overwhelmed within me; my heart within me is desolate.

I remember the days of old; I meditate on all thy works; I muse on the work of thy hands.

I stretch forth my hands unto thee: my soul thirsteth after thee, as a thirsty land. Selah.

Hear me speedily, O Lord: my spirit faileth: hide not thy face from me, lest I be like unto them that go down into the pit.

Cause me to hear thy lovingkindness in the morning; for in thee do I trust: cause me to know the way wherein I should walk; for I lift up my soul unto thee.

Deliver me, O LORD, from mine enemies: I flee unto thee to hide me.

Teach me to do thy will; for thou art my God: thy spirit is good; lead me into the land of uprightness.

Quicken me, O LORD, for thy name's sake: for thy righteousness' sake bring my soul out of trouble.

And of thy mercy cut off mine enemies, and destroy all them that afflict my soul: for I am thy servant.

To contact the Author:

Melinda Turner

mturnerrn@charter.net

Please allow this book to be a blessing to you. I would love to read your testimony.

97506660R00114

Made in the USA
Columbia, SC
17 June 2018